MAPS and
MAPPING the WORLD

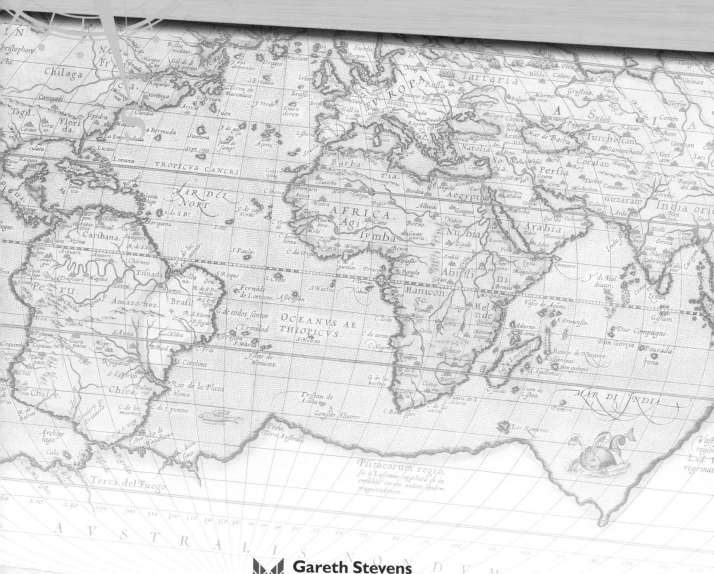

Gareth Stevens
Publishing

Please visit our Web site www.garethstevens.com. For a free color catalog of all our high-quality books, call toll free 1-800-542-2595 or fax 1-877-542-2596.

Library of Congress Cataloging-in-Publication Data
Understanding maps of our world : maps and mapping the world / Ben Hollingum, editor.
    p. cm.
      Includes index.
      ISBN 978-1-4339-3498-8 (library binding) — ISBN 978-1-4339-3501-5 (pbk.)
      ISBN 978-1-4339-3502-2 (6-pack)
      I. Hollingum, Ben.
   GA105.3.U54 2010
   912—dc22   009037275

Published in 2010 by
Gareth Stevens Publishing
111 East 14th Street, Suite 349
New York, NY 10003

© 2010 The Brown Reference Group Ltd.

For Gareth Stevens Publishing:
Art Direction: Haley Harasymiw
Editorial Direction: Kerri O'Donnell

For The Brown Reference Group Ltd:
Editorial Director: Lindsey Lowe
Managing Editor: Tim Cooke
Children's Publisher: Anne O'Daly
Design Manager: David Poole
Designer: Simon Morse
Production Director: Alastair Gourlay
Picture Manager: Sophie Mortimer
Picture Researcher: Clare Newman

Picture Credits:
Front Cover: DigitalVision; NASA br

Brown Reference Group: all artwork

Corbis: Bettmann 31; The Gallery Collection 30; The Picture Desk Ltd 39; DigitalVision: 4m, 4b, 25; iStock: Lisa Klump 12; Jupiter Images: Ablestock 5m, 32; Photos.com 28; Stockxpert 5t; NASA: 9; Landsat 10l, 10r; Shutterstock: Ajay Bhaskar 26b; Eric Geveart 43; Glyphstock 41; Vladislav Gurfinkel 4t; Jeremy Richards 26t; Dave Rock 23; Rose Armin 42; Veronika Vasilyuk 20; Steven Wright 5b; Gary Yim 7

Publisher's note to educators and parents: Our editors have carefully reviewed the Web sites that appear on p. 46 to ensure that they are suitable for students. Many Web sites change frequently, however, and we cannot guarantee that a site's future contents will continue to meet our high standards of quality and educational value. Be advised that students should be closely supervised whenever they access the Internet.

Manufactured in the United States of America
1 2 3 4 5 6 7 8 9   12 11 10

CPSIA compliance information: Batch #BRW0102GS: For further information contact Gareth Stevens, New York, New York at 1-800-542-2595.

Contents

The Changing Shape of the World

1400

This map shows the world known to Europeans in the fifteenth century: Europe and parts of Asia and Africa.

1700

1600

In this seventeenth-century map, only the interior of North America and the southern oceans remain empty.

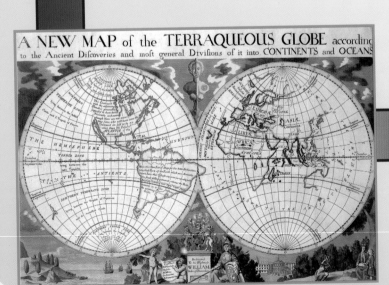

1800

This map reveals more information about Australia, but the northwest coast of North America and most of the Pacific Ocean remain unknown.

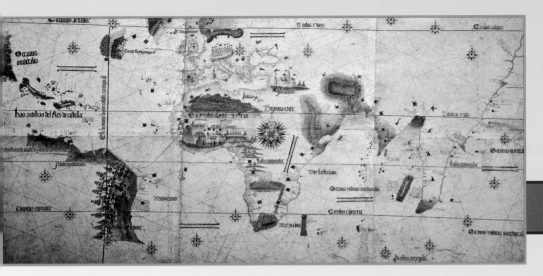

This sixteenth-century map fills in the coasts of Africa and India, the Caribbean islands, and parts of South America.

1500

In this sixteenth-century map, South America is only roughly shaped; the northwest coast of Australia has become part of the legendary "southern continent."

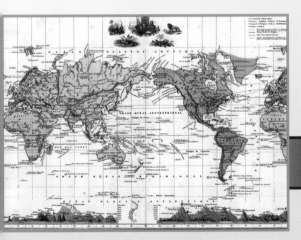

The first photographs of Earth from space were taken only in the 1960s.

1900

This world map was drawn in 1875, when Europeans were at the height of claiming colonies in other lands.

Introduction

This is a volume from the set Understanding Maps of Our World. This book looks at how maps and mapping help travelers find their way.

UNDERSTANDING MAPS OF OUR WORLD IS AN eight-volume set that describes the history of cartography, discusses its importance in different cultures, and explains how it is done. Cartography is the technique of compiling information for, and then drawing, maps or charts. Each volume in the set examines a particular aspect of mapping and uses numerous artworks and photographs to help the reader understand the sometimes complex themes.

After all, cartography is both a science and an art. It has existed since before words were written down and today uses the most up-to-date computer technology and imaging systems. Advances in mapmaking through history have been closely involved with wider advances in science and technology. Studying maps demands some understanding of math and at the same time an appreciation of visual creativity. Such a subject is bound to get a little complex at times!

About this Book

This volume considers how human beings have looked at the world in the past and the maps they have produced. Each person's view of the world is different, and that means that many different maps are created. These maps do not have to take the form of pictures, they can be kept in a person's memory and passed on through stories or songs. The modern use of photographs of the earth, especially from the air, has made maps more accurate and standardized, but there are still possibilities for new maps to be made by creative people. Maps do not just show features in the landscape: It is important to understand the difference between topographic and thematic maps.

 Nobody likes to feel lost. With accurate modern maps, people can travel vast distances and still know where they are in relation to their home. In the past, people rarely traveled beyond their home town.

LONDON 13,740

PARIS

MADRID 12,726 k

NEW YORK 11,168 km

RIO DE JANEIRO 4,6

The Earth from Space

Long before humans ventured into space they had begun to think of the Earth as viewed from above. That allowed them to represent places on a flat surface: on a map.

IMAGINE BEING AN ASTRONAUT: LOOKING DOWN AT OUR BLUE-green planet from an orbiting spacecraft. The scenes you see might be very complex—intricate coastlines and varying patterns of vegetation. In some places you might be able to see the effect of human beings on our planet. You could probably spot clearings in the South American rain forest. There might be pollution clouds in the air from factories. At night you could see the pattern of lights showing towns and cities.

All of these features of the Earth's surface can be measured and put on maps. Even features in the atmosphere, like cloud patterns, and things on the seabed (invisible to us on dry land) can be measured and presented on a map. A map is the best way of storing all this information about the Earth. To help make sense of the complicated world we live in, people have used maps for centuries.

Looking Down

Very early in human history people had the idea of making lines and pictures—perhaps on a rock or part of a cave wall—to represent a very big object—sometimes even the whole world. Early people were able, just as we are today, to have a picture of the world in their mind. It could help them in remembering what was over the next hilltop, or it could be their view of what the world as a whole might look like—though they could not see or measure it as we can. They could draw that picture as a map.

Maps are particular views of the world, and one of their special characteristics is that they are views from above, looking downward. That is a surprising viewpoint for early humans to have because none of them could have seen the world from above. But it is important to imagine this viewpoint because making maps depends on it. To see large areas of the world, you need, really, to put yourself in the position of the astronaut. To see over the hill, you need to have the viewpoint of a bird.

This satellite photograph of the Earth is effectively a photographic map of North and South America, the Caribbean, and the Pacific Ocean. It has had its colors enhanced to show features such as the dry coastal strip of Peru and Chile. A pinwheel-shaped hurricane swirls in the Gulf of Mexico.

Man-made Features

Astronauts who have traveled far away from Earth are able to see a complete hemisphere (half of the world) at one glance. However, they cannot see many individual features on the surface of the Earth. The biggest man-made features visible from space are the polders of the Netherlands in Europe. A polder is an area of land that has been reclaimed from the sea by draining it and by building walls to keep the sea out. The polders have allowed the country to increase its total land area by a fifth. When you travel closer and closer to the Earth from space, you are able to pick out more features you can identify and include on a map.

Zooming in

All maps (except star maps) take a bird's-eye view of an area; they look down. Since the invention of the airplane, photograph has been able to use the bird's-eye view to produce maps.

FROM A COMMERCIAL JET AT MAXIMUM ALTITUDE, WHICH can be 6 or 7 miles (10 km) above Earth, you can see mainly natural features such as forests, oceans, and deserts. Maps that show whole countries include these features. As the airplane descends, more and more of the human world can be seen—cities, highways, farms and their field patterns, harbors, and airports. As you come down further, you reach a point where you get the same view as a bird. You can see the pattern of streets in the neighborhood and individual buildings.

What you have been looking at during your journey from the moon or your descent in an airplane are all the features that are included on the maps of your neighborhood that you can buy or look at in your local

⊙ **The polders of the Netherlands. Drainage work has been carried out since medieval times and has transformed marshy areas, mud flats, and some shallow coastal waters into usable agricultural and settled land.**

⊙ **Most larger polders are used for agriculture, and field patterns are noticeable from infrared satellite images like this. More than one-third of the Netherlands is below sea level.**

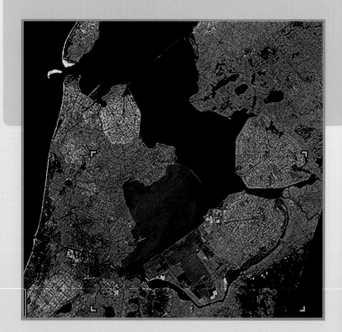

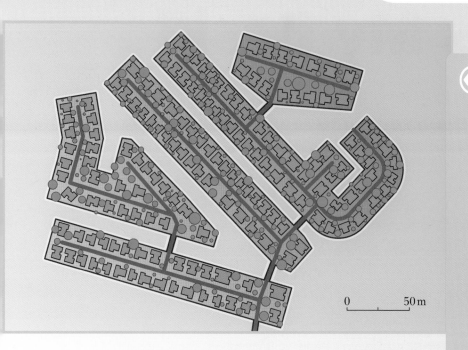

This map of Fort Lauderdale is a "straight down" view of a neighborhood, based on a photograph taken from the air. Symbols show the trees, houses, roads, and bridges. The blue background is a deliberate color choice because—like the polders on page 10—this neighborhood has been built on "reclaimed" land. It is in the middle of the shallow Stanahan River.

0   50m

library. Cities, highways, street patterns, shopping centers, parks, schools, factories, your house, and your yard will all be on a map. In fact, they will probably be on several different maps.

Map Scale

If there are lots of buildings, streets, and parks on the map, and they are shown very small, then the map is a "small-scale" map. Small-scale maps usually show quite a large area. If the map you are looking at shows only a part of your neighborhood, but the buildings are shown quite large, and the streets are quite wide, then you have a "large-scale" map.

It is possible to make a map of your area by going into it and surveying all the objects on the ground. That usually involves expensive equipment that can measure very accurately. However, organizations and companies that take aerial photographs from aircraft with special cameras are more likely to have produced the types of maps that show your local area. All the measurements needed for the map can be taken from the aerial photographs instead of on the ground.

The pictures taken from an airplane, like the "bird's-eye view," are views from straight above looking straight down. The map is made from the photograph, but it is better in many ways for showing things that you cannot see on the photograph, such as street names.

That's My Desk!

Imagine you are producing a simple map of your schoolroom. If you stand at the front of the room, you have a reasonable view over the room but you cannot see everything.

YOU CAN PROBABLY SEE ALL THE DESKS AND OTHER furniture in the room. Though there might be some bookshelves, for example, on the wall behind you. Also, your view of the desks in front of you is an oblique view. You can see the top and the fronts of the desks only, and the chairs are hidden behind the desks from your viewpoint.

If you are preparing a map, you need to imagine yourself, instead, looking straight down at all the desks and chairs, your teacher's table, and the other pieces of furniture in the room.

The map will be a large-scale map. It will cover a small area—just the schoolroom—and even small features, like a wastebasket and a computer, can be shown on it. You will be able to put your own desk on the map as an identifiable object.

To produce this map, you must measure the sizes of these features and the distance from one feature to another. These

A school classroom viewed from an "oblique" eye-level viewpoint. It is not possible to see all the objects in the classroom from this angle.

12

This map of a classroom is a "straight down" view. It allows you to see all the tables and monitors, along with the location of features that would be hidden in a photograph, like the wastebaskets, the blackboard, and the doors.

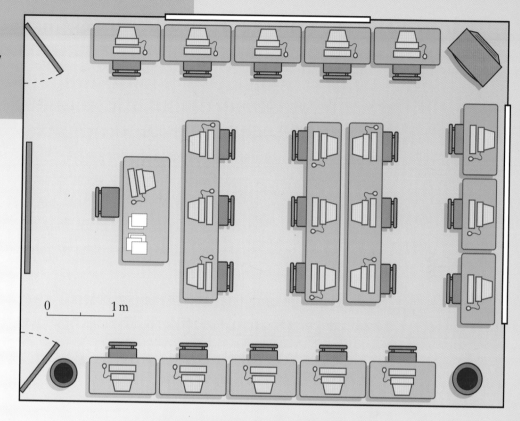

measurements can be scaled and plotted onto a piece of paper or on a computer screen. You may decide that a distance of 1 centimeter on the map will represent a distance of 1 meter (100 centimeters) in the real world. The scale of this map is written as 1:100 and described as "one to one hundred" or "one over one hundred." This means that one unit of measurement on the map is equivalent to 100 units of measurement in the real world.

The first measurements to make are the lengths of the walls, since everything else will be mapped inside the shape of the room. If the room is a regular shape, you can plot the measurements easily on a sheet of graph paper or squared paper. Most of the furniture will also be rectangular and easy to measure and plot. As long as the map does not become too crowded or difficult to read, you can also add your own ideas. You could show the position of your desk, for example, by drawing it in a different color and adding a label.

Photographs and Maps

A photograph of an object shows all the detail, but a drawing of the same object highlights the aspects that the artist thinks are important.

IF YOU DRAW THE VIEW OF YOUR CLASSROOM FROM ABOVE, you can highlight the edges of objects, like tables or chairs, using lines (see page 13). You can also produce a drawing that emphasizes certain objects by coloring in areas. In a similar way, aerial photographs of a landscape are different from maps of the same area because the mapmaker chooses what to emphasize. The maps may concentrate on features in the landscape such as lines (like roads or fences) or areas (like lakes or forests).

Many maps use both lines and shaded or colored areas, along with symbols at certain points, like railroad crossings or mountain summits. Together they create a representation of the real world that is a picture, not a photograph.

Advantages and Disadvantages

The labels on the photographs (right) show the advantages of a photograph in giving information. The labels on the maps indicate examples of things that maps can show better than photographs.

The mapmaker has taken measurements from the aerial photograph of the city and created the map you can see alongside. The types of buildings, here the hotel and post office, are shown in words, and the pattern of the roads is much clearer.

You cannot see on the map of the agricultural area that one of the bottom fields has been plowed. Unless you check the area symbols for the map, you would never guess that the light green color showed woods, something you can easily see in the photograph. But the map makes it much easier to see the field boundaries.

The infrared photograph of the tidal zone shows sand, grasses, salt meadows, and marsh. It is a difficult scene to map. The mapmaker has decided to use area symbols and to highlight deep channels of water.

Editing Visual Information. Different types of landscape produce different scenes in aerial photographs. Many features on the photographs are ignored or modified when a map of the area is drawn. The map can highlight features and simplify complex photographs.

Urban landscape

Urban vegetation

Heights of some buildings

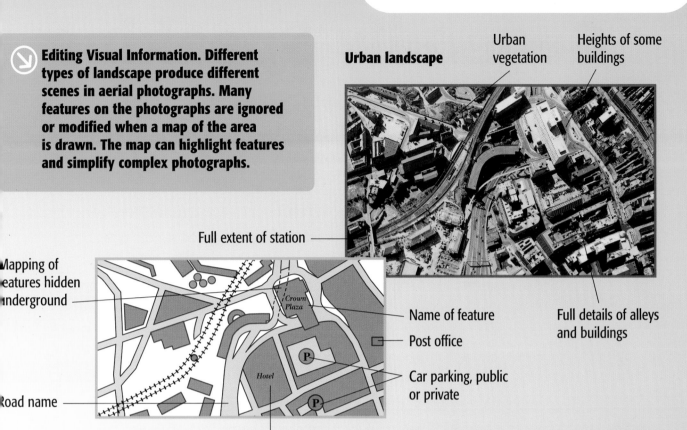

Mapping of features hidden underground

Full extent of station

Name of feature

Post office

Car parking, public or private

Full details of alleys and buildings

Road name

Type of building

Agricultural landscape

Woodland

Natural landscape

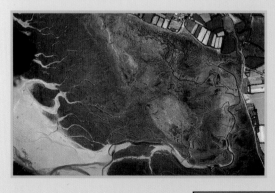

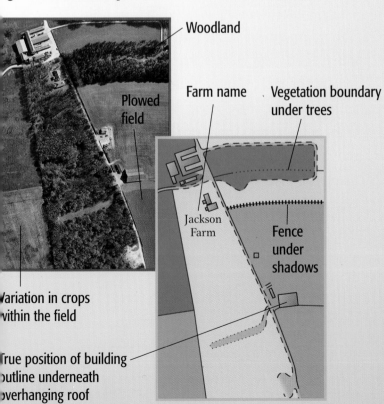

Plowed field

Farm name

Vegetation boundary under trees

Jackson Farm

Fence under shadows

Variation in crops within the field

True position of building outline underneath overhanging roof

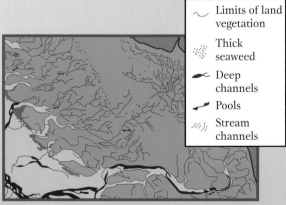

	Limits of land vegetation
	Thick seaweed
	Deep channels
	Pools
	Stream channels

Generally Speaking

As we have seen, an aerial photograph shows all the complicated detail of a landscape, while a map tries to show only the important features.

THE SMALLER THE SCALE OF THE MAP, THE MORE ESSENTIAL it is to ensure that the way features are highlighted is not confusing. The technique of making sure that the map is simplified as the scale gets smaller is called generalization. There are several different things that a mapmaker can do when generalizing a map. First, leave out the minor elements. A map of an area may leave out many minor roads and tracks and show only the more important connecting highways.

Second, emphasize some features, making them more obvious on the map than they are in the real world. So, to make sure the highways can be seen clearly, some may be drawn much wider than the rivers on the same map. In the real world the rivers may be wider.

Generalization simplifies the real world. The rivers on the maps here have many more bends and curves than shown. The mapmaker has smoothed the line to give an impression of the river, rather than a true-to-life representation. The detail of the city area on the map (lower right) has been generalized to indicate it is an urban type of landscape. The person reading the map is expected to understand the nature of the real world by interpreting the map.

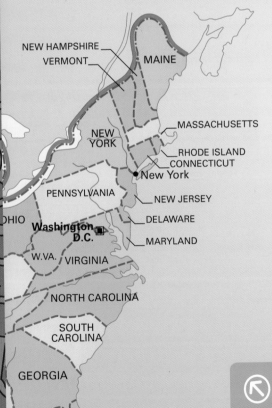

NEW HAMPSHIRE
VERMONT
MAINE
MASSACHUSETTS
NEW YORK
RHODE ISLAND
CONNECTICUT
New York
PENNSYLVANIA
NEW JERSEY
DELAWARE
OHIO
Washington D.C.
MARYLAND
W.VA. VIRGINIA
NORTH CAROLINA
SOUTH CAROLINA
GEORGIA
FLORIDA

Small Scale. This map of the eastern United States shows very little detail. The only features are the coastline, the location of big cities, and the states.

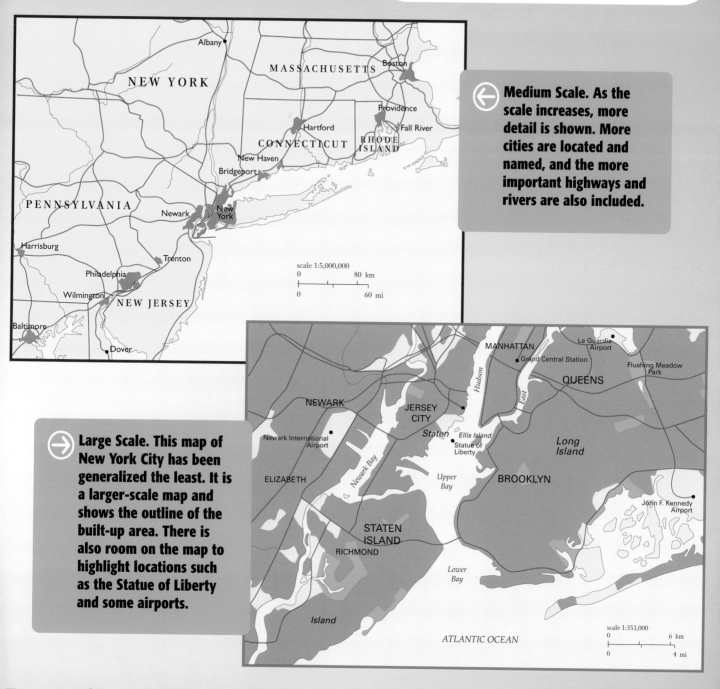

Medium Scale. As the scale increases, more detail is shown. More cities are located and named, and the more important highways and rivers are also included.

scale 1:5,000,000

Large Scale. This map of New York City has been generalized the least. It is a larger-scale map and shows the outline of the built-up area. There is also room on the map to highlight locations such as the Statue of Liberty and some airports.

scale 1:353,000

Topographic and Thematic Maps

Each of the maps on pages 16 and 17 is a topographic map. They are maps that show the landscape and what is on it. The largest-scale topographic maps are created using large-scale aerial photographs. These maps are then generalized in order to create smaller-scale maps.

A thematic map that provides information about the weather or history or the roads also has to be generalized. A road map may just show the positions of towns and the coastline along with the roads.

Making Symbols

If a map has to emphasize features and perhaps show them as more prominent on the map than they are to scale in the real world, then symbols are used for those features.

THERE ARE FOUR MAIN TYPES OF SYMBOLS THAT CAN BE used on a map. The first type are "point" symbols used to stand for features that exist at exact locations in the real world, like a mountain peak, a campsite, or a bus stop. For small-scale maps even towns and cities could be shown by point symbols because they are such small features compared to the large area that a very small-scale map covers. The point symbols can be simple geometrical shapes, such as dots, circles, or squares, or they can be more like little pictures of a mountain, a tent, or a bus.

The second type of symbol on a map is the "line" symbol. Line symbols are used to represent rivers and coastlines—physical features—but they can also

➔ **This map is designed with point and line symbols. They can represent a wide range of features in the landscape. It does not give as much information as the map of the same area on the right; but because it shows less, it is easier to read.**

ℂ Telephone	🚐 Caravan site
♜ Castle	🗼 Lighthouse
📡 TV or radio mast	══ Secondary road
✗ Windmill	══ Main road
♁ Church	══ Highway
☼ Ancient site	—·—·— District boundary
℗ Car park	-------- Footpath
	—— Railway line

represent boundaries such as state lines or country frontiers. Lines can be solid or dotted. They can also be drawn in different thicknesses. The major highway in the illustrations on these pages has one thick blue line and two more black lines on either side.

"Area" symbols show features like marshes, lakes, and city zones. The most common area symbols are just one color, such as a blue symbol for the sea and yellow for sand. Some of them include a little more decoration, like the symbols for trees used here that have a simple picture of the tree type drawn on them.

The final type of symbol used on maps is text—written letters and numbers. The map on the right tells us that a particular river is called "Red Deer Creek" and that the hill in the top left corner is 355 feet high.

Color, Shape, and Size

Different colors represent different features—often blue for water, green for vegetation, and brown for landscape.

Point symbols have different shapes, such as the circular "ancient site" symbol and the triangular height indicators here.

Another variation can be in size. The circle representing a small village may the same shape and color as the symbol representing a large city, but would be smaller on the map.

Every map has a legend (sometimes called a key) that shows all the symbols and tells the map reader what they mean.

This map has more features represented by symbols. Area symbols have been added along with some text. As long as a map has a "key" or "legend" to explain the meaning of the symbols, the mapmaker is free to design an attractive map.

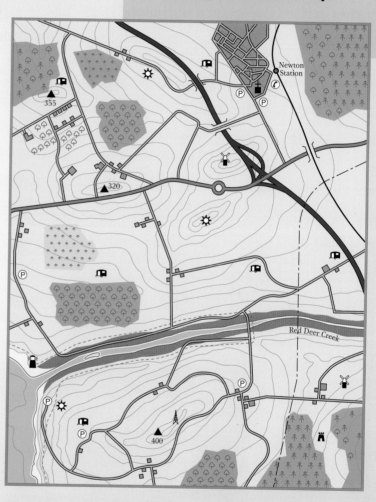

	Nonconiferous trees		Sea
	Coniferous trees		Sand
	Bushes		Mud
	Orchard		

Material for Maps

The maps that you are familiar with from your school atlas or from TV weather forecasts look very different than some of the older maps in this book.

THE REASON FOR THESE DIFFERENCES IS THAT THE methods and materials used to produce maps have changed so much since the first ones were made thousands of years ago. Maps still rely on measurements of the world, as they always have done, but the way in which these measurements are presented has gradually changed.

It is difficult to know when true cartography (mapmaking) started. The earliest diagrams that definitely represent real features like paths, streams, and trees can be dated to about 3000 B.C. and were carved on rock faces.

Maps from the Near East (in present-day Iran and Iraq) from about 1500 B.C. were carved onto wet clay tablets that were then dried in the sun. Many of them can be found in museums.

⬇ **Egyptian scenes of the afterlife on papyrus, from 1100 B.C. The lines are still sharp after all that time.**

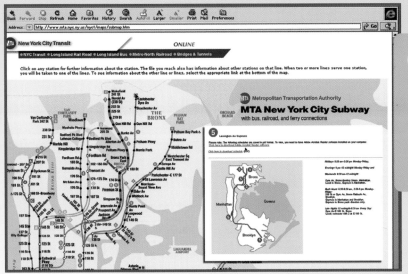

Most maps today are produced on computer screens, like this subway map delivered using the World Wide Web. The Internet makes looking for maps much easier than it was when only books could be consulted.

Maps in colored ink drawn on rolls of papyrus, invented in Egypt, were not so long lasting. Papyrus is made from a type of reed grown in marshy areas. The great advantages of papyrus, apart from greater clarity and accuracy, were lightness and flexibility.

From as early as 200 B.C. maps were drawn on a material made of cleaned, stretched animal skins. It was called parchment. (A fine kind of parchment, made of the best skins of calves and young goats, was called vellum.) Parchment was still being used for books many centuries later, in the Middle Ages.

Paper was invented in China and was not introduced to the rest of the world until A.D. 610. It is still the most common method of producing hard-copy, printed maps. In the 1800s the introduction of specialized printing techniques meant that instead of each map being hand drawn, one map could be reproduced in thousands of copies, all exactly the same.

Today most maps are drawn on computer screens. These maps are different from printed maps because they disappear when the computer is switched off! They are called soft-copy or temporary maps. Using up-to-date computer programs, it is possible to draw high-quality maps without having to sketch the map in freehand. The maps still contain the point, line, area, and text symbols that all maps have contained for thousands of years. But they have been drawn by computer and are presented on screens that would have astonished our ancestors.

The Earliest Maps

Since the earliest maps were created thousands of years ago, they have continued to help people make sense of their surroundings.

THE FIRST MAPS DID INCLUDE INFORMATION ABOUT things like rivers and forests, like a modern map. But they also must have helped people feel as if they understood the world a little better. The earliest people must have found the world a frightening place, full of things they could not explain. Anything that helped make sense of it—like a map—was welcome.

Maps have been produced for longer than languages or numbers have been written down, so they are one of the oldest forms of human communication. Mapping is a natural human skill—certainly no other animals can do it! (Though some creatures seem to have extremely accurate "mental maps" of the world, like birds that migrate over thousands of miles.)

These ancient peoples produced three types of maps. First, there were maps of the area in which they lived. They were usually based on the walking distances that tribes recorded.

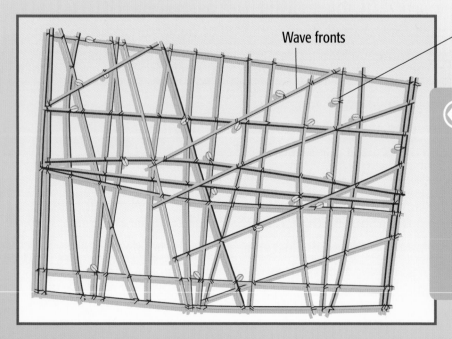

Wave fronts

Islands indicated by shells

← This map of ocean currents and islands was made out of reeds. It comes from the South Pacific and helped people traveling in dugout canoes and outriggers to find their way from island to island.

It might take, for example, half a day to reach a spring used as a water source. A hunting ground might actually be the same distance away, but it might take two day's hike across mountains to reach it. The map would represent the time measurement rather than the distance measurement.

Some early Neolithic diagrams (from 5000 B.C.) show symbols, sometimes people or animals; they also show some generalization. These early maps were produced on permanent surfaces like rock faces, so they are unlikely to have been used for navigation. Instead, they were probably used for ceremonies and acted as symbols for the tribe. They helped give a feeling of belonging, of being "at home."

The second type of map was of the sky—the stars, planets, and their changing patterns. They are not true maps because they have no proper scale, but they do accurately show the relationships between objects in the night sky.

The final type of map was not drawn as a result of observation. It was based on stories and myths, especially about how the Earth was created. These cosmological maps are described in the next section.

Explaining the Universe

Early peoples felt that their day-to-day lives depended on the continuous working of nature in patterns that had been established by gods or the processes of creation.

IF THE WORLD COULD BE POSITIONED ON A MAP THAT showed those processes, perhaps it would be easier to avoid disaster, or at least to understand why it happened. People thought that interruptions to day-to-day life like thunderstorms, earthquakes, eclipses, planetary movements, and plagues needed to be explained, and order needed to be restored. Rituals such as sacrifices and worship were intended to reestablish order. The real world was not just made up of trees and rivers and animals. It included the relationship between the Earth (and humankind which lived on it) and the rest of the universe.

Many myths grew up about the creation of the world, and they had a significant effect on the way different peoples viewed the world. The creation stories explained how the land, sea, and sky were created and how human beings came into existence. Creation stories varied, and any maps based on them also varied. These mythological stories that explained the creation and place of the Earth existed in all cultures.

Some Chinese and Japanese accounts suggested the universe was something like an egg—the yolk representing the Earth and the surrounding white representing the mysterious "waters" of the heavens. The mythical story of Pan-ku, the Chinese primeval man, is a development of the egg legend. Eighteen thousand years after being born from the original cosmic egg, Pan-ku died. His head formed the sun and moon. His blood became the water on the Earth's surface. His sweat formed the rain. His hair created the forests, and his breath produced the winds. And the fleas that lived on his body became the ancestors of human beings!

ORBIUM PLA
TERRAM COM
TIUM SCENO

NETARUM
PLECTEN
GRAPHIA.

SPHÆRA ZODIACI
SPHÆRA SATVRNI
SPHÆRA IOVIS
SPHÆRA MARTIS
SPHÆRA SOLIS
SPHÆRA VENERIS
SPHÆRA MERCVRII
SPHÆRA LVNÆ

CIRCVLVS
CAPRI CORNVS
AQVA RIVS
PI SCES
ÆQVINOCTIALIS
GEME NI
TAV RVS
ARI ES
SCOR PIVS

HYPOTHESIS PTOLEMAICA,
in quâ Terra totius Universi
fit centrum.

↑ **This eighteenth-century map reconstructs the plan of the universe as seen by Greek astronomers. The Earth is at the center, orbited by the planets, moon, and sun.**

Layers and Shapes

As human societies developed, they began to consider the arrangement of the features of the world. An early idea was of "layers." The Sumerian peoples, creators of one of the earliest civilizations, lived about 5,000 years ago where the Tigris and Euphrates rivers meet (now in southern Iraq). They thought that the Earth had a layer underneath, a vast underground reservoir, which fed the rivers and kept them flowing even when no rain fell.

Ancient Egyptians thought that the sky was a layer above the Earth supported on four giant pillars.

Some other civilizations imagined circles and spheres instead of flat layers. Both Hindu philosophy in India and the much later Roman civilization thought of the universe as a series of spheres fitted inside each other. Early Judaism shared a similar view of the sky as a solid spherical dome with window holes through which rain fell.

All the maps drawn from these stories and beliefs were simple diagrams that represented the whole of the universe and the Earth, with the Earth normally the biggest part. In order to make maps based on these views more convincing, some of the real objects in the world were included, like the sea and the mountain ranges.

Observations and Calculations

As civilizations developed, maps came to rely less and less on the imagination and more and more on what people could see with their own eyes. While the priests and philosophers were thinking about the structure of the universe in a philosophical way, some people were making practical

Ancient Indian observatories still stand in cities such as Jaipur. Buildings like this observation platform were designed to line up with heavenly bodies so that calculations could be made about the movement of stars.

The ancient observatory at New Delhi, India. The 13 astronomical instruments, including a giant sun dial, were built to help improve the calendar through the precise measurement of heavenly movement and the prediction of astronomical events.

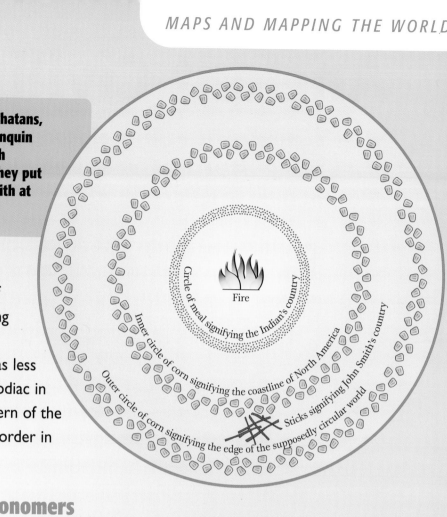

> → **The world as seen by the Powhatans, Native Americans whose Algonquin group took Captain John Smith prisoner in Virginia in 1607. They put the home of stranger John Smith at the edge of the world.**

Fire

Circle of meal signifying the Indian's country

Inner circle of corn signifying the coastline of North America

Outer circle of corn signifying the edge of the supposedly circular world

Sticks signifying John Smith's country

observations. The pattern of stars was recognized as being permanent, although the movement of the planets was less constant. The signs of the Zodiac in the sky and the regular pattern of the seasons suggested a natural order in the universe.

Some Important Astronomers

This new science influenced the development from about 500 B.C. of Greek cartography. The Greeks assumed the planets moved around the perfectly spherical Earth and that these orbits were also perfectly circular and predictable.

Scientific observations continued through the centuries. The Polish astronomer Copernicus (1473–1543), the German Johannes Kepler (1571–1630), and Galileo (1564–1642), who lived in Italy, based their views of the universe on their observations of the sky and mathematical calculations. Copernicus was the first to suggest that the Earth orbits around the sun, rather than the other way around. Kepler figured out that the orbits of the planets are elliptical, rather than circular. And Galileo made important discoveries about the moons that orbit other planets in predictable ways.

Today maps are made using measurements and photographs of the world, and it is only some of the remaining aboriginal tribes who view the Earth and its place in the universe in the same way as our ancestors did thousands of years ago.

Ancient Civilizations

In the ancient world aspects of learning and technology that would be important for mapmaking developed at different rates in different societies.

PAPER AND A GRID SYSTEM FOR POSITIONING THINGS on it would come from the East. The idea of map projections would come from the West.

In areas of Europe and around the Mediterranean important civilizations grew up from about 2500 B.C. On the banks of the Nile River the ancient Egyptian society flourished and was able to undertake extraordinary feats of construction. The famous Great Pyramids at Giza, near Cairo, were built from 2700 B.C. to 1000 B.C. Such work required accurate measurements.

In addition, the Egyptians needed to measure land boundaries and find out who owned each piece of land so that fields and farms could be marked out. Every year the annual flood of the Nile River washed away the boundary markers, so the legal owners needed to be recorded in some way. Both construction and land recording needed well-trained surveyors and mapmakers to measure positions on the ground and keep registers in the form of maps.

⊙→ **An engraving of the goddess Urania (Greek goddess of astronomy) inspiring the geographer Ptolemy in his work. He is using a sextant to find the position of the stars.**

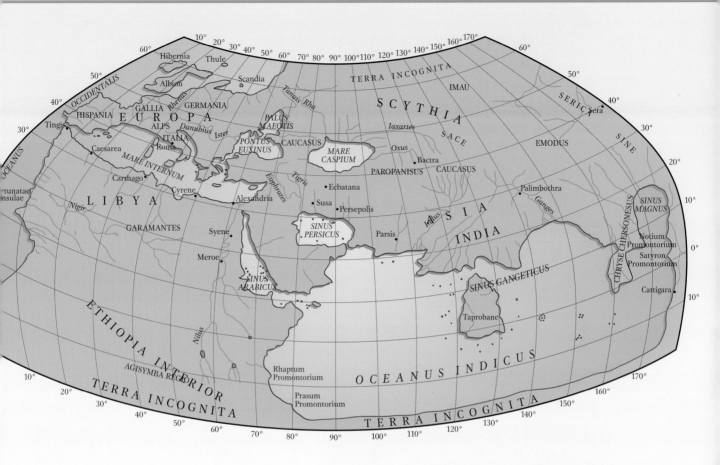

The map shows various geographical labels including: Hibernia, Thule, Scandia, Albion, OCCIDENTALIS, Rhenus, GERMANIA, HISPANIA, GALLIA, EUROPA, ALPS, Danubius Ister, Tanais Rha, TERRA INCOGNITA, SCYTHIA, IMAU, SERICA Sera, Tingis, ITALIA, Roma, PALUS MAEOTIS, PONTUS EUXINUS, CAUCASUS, Iaxartes, SACE, EMODUS, SINE, Caesarea, MARE INTERNUM, MARE CASPIUM, Oxus, Bactra, CAUCASUS, Carthago, PAROPANISUS, OCEANUS, Cyrene, Euphrates, Tigris, Ecbatana, Palimbothra, fortunatae insulae, LIBYA, Alexandria, Susa, Persepolis, ASIA, Ganges, SINUS MAGNUS, Niger, SINUS PERSICUS, Parsis, INDIA, CHRYSE CHERSONESUS, Notium Promontorium, GARAMANTES, Syene, Indus, Satyron Promontorium, Meroe, Cattigara, SINUS ARABICUS, SINUS GANGETICUS, ETHIOPIA INTERIOR, Taprobane, Nilus, AGISYMBA REGIO, OCEANUS INDICUS, Rhaptum Promontorium, TERRA INCOGNITA, Prasum Promontorium, TERRA INCOGNITA

↑ **A reconstruction of a map by Ptolemy showing most of Europe and large parts of Africa and Asia. The Greeks thought that the Indian Ocean (Oceanus Indicus) was surrounded by land. When the Americas were discovered 1,400 years after Ptolemy, his projection method was used to map them.**

Much of the wealth of the kingdoms along the Nile came from gold mines in the hills bordering the Red Sea to the east. They were important to the Egyptian kings, and plans of their gold mines have been discovered in some of their tombs. Other more personal maps were also placed within the graves underneath pyramids. Maps have been found showing the route to the "afterlife" to be used by the spirits of the dead kings. They form part of the Books of the Dead, which were meant to be guides to the "afterlife."

Practical Use and Theory Combine

Egyptian influence over the eastern Mediterranean region was enormous for a very long period. It was not until Alexander the Great invaded in 332 B.C. that Egypt started to absorb the ideas of other civilizations. By that time Greek philosophers had developed theories about the shape of the Earth and the outlines of the land and sea. Many of the Greeks believed that nature was perfect and that the precise form of the Earth therefore had to be the perfect shape, a sphere. That seemed to be confirmed by looking at the curved shadow of the Earth on the moon during an eclipse.

The importance of observations and measurement became more and more clear to the Greeks during the period from 500 B.C. to the time of Ptolemy, the most famous Greek geographer. Ptolemy, who lived from A.D. 90 to A.D. 168, did not only make maps. He also wrote books on how to make maps and prepared lists of information (most importantly, the locations of towns in the ancient world) that could be used in mapmaking.

He was one of the first cartographers to find out how to show the sphere on a flat piece of paper, using map projections. The map on this page shows his projection and the kind of information that he was able to put on his maps. He suggested ways of dividing up the world so that maps of countries and smaller regions could be produced.

The Greek cartographers did not create large numbers of maps to be used for practical tasks, as the Egyptians did. They wanted to record the whole world, and their writings and the maps that have survived show the extent of Western geographical knowledge at the beginning of the first millennium.

This fifteenth-century map shows the British Isles and Ireland according to the projection proposed by Ptolemy. The projection distorts the shape of Scotland (top) and of southwest England (bottom).

This faded map of a palace complex is from a Korean atlas, but the writing in the atlas is all Chinese. The "Yojido" atlas was produced in the 1760s.

Eastern Civilizations

Tools for measurement and for preparing maps in China became advanced long before they did in the Western civilizations around the Mediterranean. Paper had replaced wooden strips by the fourth century B.C., long before its use in the West.

The early astronomer Chang Heng introduced the idea of a map based on a grid system that allows you to read locations off the map easily. This rectangular system is still used today.

A Chinese engineer, Phei Hsiu, who lived in the third century A.D., wrote instruction books on how to make maps. He also created a list of names (called a gazetteer) of important places throughout China and prepared some up-to-date maps covering the whole country. Phei Hsiu used techniques of land surveying and map plotting that were not used in Western civilizations for many centuries.

Maps in 3-D

As we know, the real world has high and low points in it (three-dimensional), while the map that results from the cartographer's design is two-dimensional.

For many centuries the only way hills and mountains were shown on maps was by symbols that looked like the landscape viewed by people on the ground. The maps had sketches of the side view of mountains. This technique was also used to represent man-made features that stood up above the Earth's surface, such as churches or castles.

Contour Lines

It was only in the 1800s that mapmakers started to show mountains on maps in the same way as all the other features—from above. To do this, they needed to invent special symbols that could show the differences in height between the valley and the mountain and show the hill slopes in the real world.

→ **This seventeenth-century map of Asia Minor (modern-day Turkey) shows mountains with sketches that are nowhere near to correct scale.**

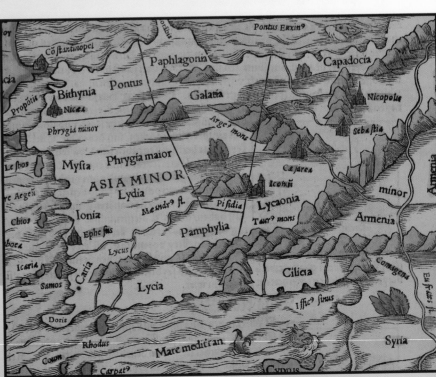

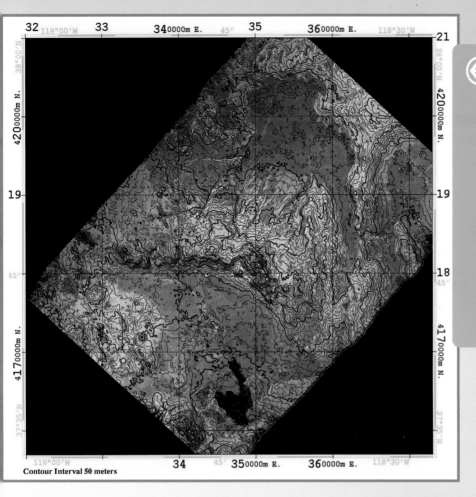

A modern map of the landscape using contours and layer tinting. Contours are lines joining places of equal height above sea level. The pattern of contour lines can represent the shape of hills and valleys. The layer tints (colored areas) also give an impression of the terrain. This map was produced using a computer.

Different symbols have been created for this. The first is the contour, a line that joins places on the ground that have the same height. The contour line shows the heights of places above sea level, which is at a height of 0 feet (meters). All mountaintops are measured, and their height above sea level is shown. If the height of any places on official or standard maps is given, it is always height above sea level.

So, the coastline drawn on a map that shows the edge of the sea has a contour value of 0. A little way inland away from the sea there will be places that are 10 feet (3 m) above sea level, and a contour line can be drawn to join these points together. All the points between this line and the coastline will be between 0 and 10 feet (0 and 3 m) above sea level, but the places on the other side of the line will all be more than 10 feet (3 m) above sea level.

As you move away from the coast, more contours can be drawn; and once you reach the mountains, there will be a complex pattern of lines that shows the height of the landscape at any position on the map.

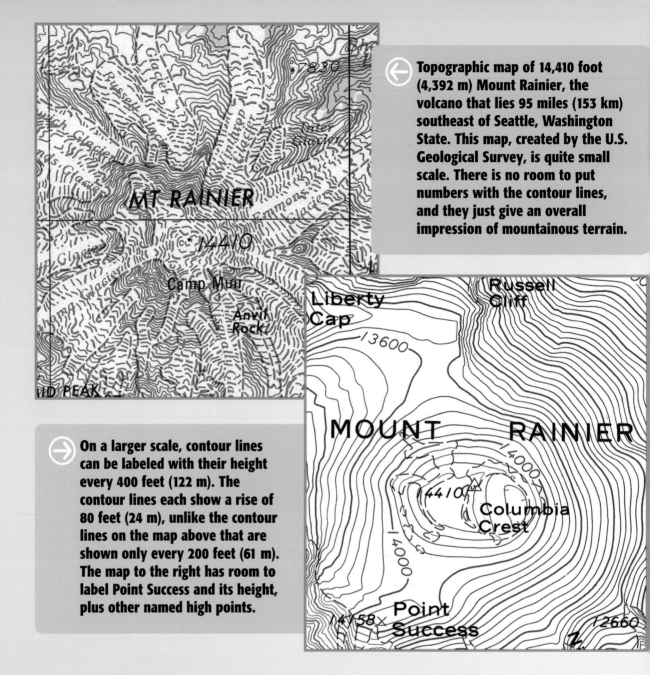

Topographic map of 14,410 foot (4,392 m) Mount Rainier, the volcano that lies 95 miles (153 km) southeast of Seattle, Washington State. This map, created by the U.S. Geological Survey, is quite small scale. There is no room to put numbers with the contour lines, and they just give an overall impression of mountainous terrain.

On a larger scale, contour lines can be labeled with their height every 400 feet (122 m). The contour lines each show a rise of 80 feet (24 m), unlike the contour lines on the map above that are shown only every 200 feet (61 m). The map to the right has room to label Point Success and its height, plus other named high points.

The arrangement of the contour lines can tell the map-reader about the landscape at a glance. Contour lines that are close together indicate a steep slope in that area, but contours that are far apart show little change in height across the area.

Shading

A second symbol used to show the landscape from above is called a hachure. It is a short line that is drawn down the slope (instead of along the slope like a contour). The hachures are thick lines where the slope is steep and are thinner where the slope is gentler. They can effectively point out steep cliffs and rock faces.

Shading that tries to show shadows on one side of a hill and brighter areas on the other side is difficult to do, but is a very effective way of showing the relief (which is the name given to the shape and appearance of the hills and valleys in the landscape). Some computer programs can now help achieve hillshading.

Tinting

Some small-scale maps, like those that show a whole continent, use a sequence of colors to show the changing relief. A common way of doing this is to use the order of colors of the rainbow. The sea is blue and the lowest land close to the coast is green. As the land rises, the colors on the map change through yellow, orange, red, and finally to purple at the highest peaks. This is called layer tinting.

A layer tinted topographical map of the United States. At this small scale it is easy to see where the highest mountains are—but it is impossible to pick out Mount Rainier.

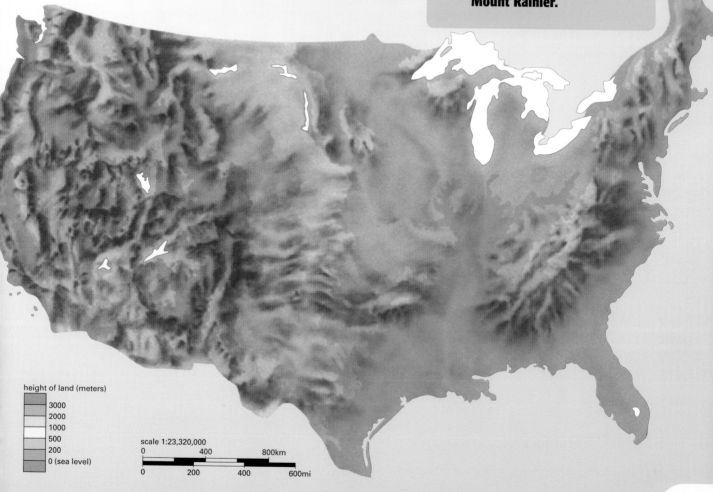

height of land (meters)

3000
2000
1000
500
200
0 (sea level)

scale 1:23,320,000

0   400   800km

0   200   400   600mi

Mapping the Invisible

As we have seen, maps can include information that a photograph cannot supply. Some maps inform us about things that can never be seen or photographed.

MANY MAPS SHOW FEATURES THAT CANNOT BE SEEN. A map of an area around an airport could plot the noise levels at different points and at different times. Such a map would be useful when planning where to locate new housing.

In fact, all maps concerned with planning could be regarded as maps of invisible things. They show what could happen in the future rather than what is currently visible in the landscape. The planned new shopping center, the revised road layout, and the altered zoning plan can all be put on a map even though they do not exist at the moment.

As well as depicting the future, maps can show features and things that existed some time in the past. We are able to produce maps to explain historical events and to recreate the times in which our ancestors lived by studying written historical records and examining archaeological evidence.

Weather maps look back and into the future. They show some features that are invisible, such as temperature, air pressure,

→ The current position of the plates on the Earth's surface; the continents have moved around the surface of the globe for 200 million years. Geologists have mapped the plates by observing features at the boundaries between them and by underground analysis.

EURASIAN PLATE
NORTH AMERICAN PLATE
CARIBBEAN PLATE
PHILIPPINE PLATE
COCOS PLATE
PACIFIC PLATE
AFRICAN PLATE
NAZCA PLATE
SOUTH AMERICAN PLATE
INDO-AUSTRALIAN PLATE
ANTARCTIC PLATE

Montréal 1760

New France

Crown Point 1759

Ticonderoga 1758

New Hampshire

Portsmouth

Fort William Henry 1756

Fort Frontenac 1758

Fort George 1756

Boston

Massachusetts

Plymouth

Fort Oswego 1756

Fort Ontario 1755

Albany

Providence

Lake Huron

Fort Rouillé

Lake Ontario

New York

Hudson

Connecticut

New Haven

Fort Niagara

Pennsylvania

New York

New Amsterdam until 1664

Ottawa

Fort St. Joseph

New Jersey

Fort Presqu'isle

Delaware

Philadelphia

Fort Pontchartrain

Lake Erie

Delaware

Lake Michigan

Fort Duquesne 1758

Baltimore

Maryland

1755

Fort Necessity

APPALACHIAN MTS

Annapolis

Miami Wyandot

Williamsburg

Virginia

ATLANTIC OCEAN

Fort St. Louis

Fort Pickawillany 1752

Richmond

Jamestown

Fort Crevecoeur

Shawnee

Ohio

Tuscarora

British settlement 1713

French settlement 1713

British settlement 1750

French settlement 1750

Fort Vincennes

Kaintuck

North Carolina

New Bern

settlement or trading post founded in the 18th century
● British
● French

Fort Chartres

Cherokee

Wilmington

French and Indian War, 1755–63
⚑ captured by British
⚑ captured by French

Mississippi

Chickasaw

South Carolina

Georgetown

⊗ British battle victory
⊗ French battle victory

Fort Prudhomme

Fort Augusta

Charleston

Ute native American peoples

Louisiana

Choctaw

Creek

Fort King George

1742

Savannah

Georgia

and wind speed, although some things, like rainfall and cloud cover are more obvious. Weather mapping relies on observations taken in many locations.

Mineral exploration companies, prospecting for metals and fuels, use sophisticated techniques to map the layers of rock beneath our feet. Their type and their folding or breaking patterns can be found out by analysis of surface and borehole rock samples taken at the site. Another method is to set off small explosions on the surface and then record the resulting sound echoes from the rocks below ground. Scientists can interpret the echo patterns to find out if an area is likely to hold oil or coal.

↑ **Maps of historical periods can be made from records and older maps. This section of a map of eastern North America in the eighteenth century pinpoints battle sites and the land occupied by Native American tribes.**

Your Worldview

Every person has his or her own view of the world. The aboriginal tribal chief has a different view from that of the scientific surveyor looking at the same mountains and valleys.

AS A RESULT IT IS DIFFICULT TO MAKE A MAP THAT DOES not show some bias and influence from the person who makes it. If you were asked to make a map of your home, for example, you might show your bedroom in great detail, but only show your brother's or your sister's bedroom as an empty outline!

Small-scale mapping is even more influenced by the mapmaker's opinions and beliefs. That is because small-scale maps show a bigger area of the real world, such as a complete country, and can only emphasize some features. You have to ask yourself: Which features are more important than others? What aspects of the country should I highlight? How should I show this country in relation to its neighbors?

Your own interpretation of the world is an important part of mapmaking. And your interpretation of the world is created and altered by many factors. For example, you may have spent some time on vacation at a seaside tourist destination in an overseas country, like Mexico or Spain. Your view of that country may not include the fact that it has mountains, deserts, and large cities because you may not have seen them yourself. Your view of the whole world is affected by your experience of traveling in it.

Both making a map and using a map are experiences that can change your worldview. Maps can help you travel; they can help you plan. Maps let us interpret the real world and give us an understanding of how we all live together on this crowded planet. Sometimes, maps can even distort the truth. Maps matter!

→ Medieval maps produced in monasteries reflected the views of monks who spent their whole lives in one place, never going beyond their cloisters and local fields. To them Jerusalem (represented by the main towers in the circle in the center of this world map) was the most important place on Earth. The monks' worldview came from their reading of the Bible and very little else.

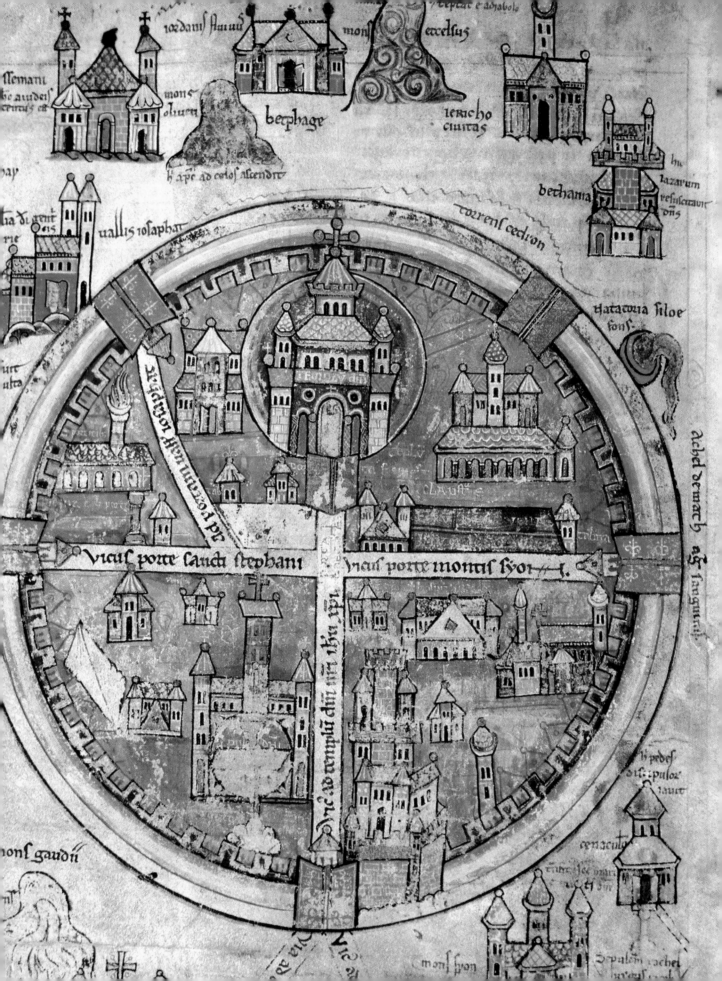

Glossary

Words in italics have their own entries in the glossary.

aborigines – the original inhabitants of an area, in particular the original inhabitants of Australia and their descendants

aerial photograph (or air photograph) – a photograph looking straight down at Earth, usually taken from an airplane, a helicopter, or a balloon

altitude – height or vertical distance above mean *sea level*; or the degrees of elevation of a star, the sun, or the moon above the horizon

ancestor – somebody from whom somebody else is directly descended; usually someone more distant than a grandparent

An aerial photograph of the crowds gathered for the inauguration of President Barack Obama in January 2009. This picture was taken from an aircraft flying below cloud-level for a better view.

atlas – a collection of maps with a uniform design bound together as a book

archaeology – the science of interpreting the past by examining remains, usually dug up from underground

astronomy – the scientific study of celestial bodies (planets and stars) and of the universe as a whole. People who do this are called astronomers.

atmosphere – the thin layer of gases around Earth

bird's-eye view – a straight-down view of Earth

Books of the Dead – Ancient Egyptian texts that were written as guides to the afterlife, containing many of the ideas of Egyptian religion. At first they were inscribed on sarcophagi (coffins) but were later written on papyrus and put with the mummy.

Earth comes between the sun and the moon (a lunar eclipse), a shadow of Earth is cast onto the moon.

elliptical – oval-shaped, like a distorted (squashed) circle; the orbits of most planets around the sun are elliptical

equator – an imaginary line running around Earth at equal distance from the North and South *Poles*. It is the line of 0 degrees *latitude*.

gazetteer – a list of names of places, with their location specified; often accompanied by a map

generalization – the task of simplifying a map, allowing it to portray the most important information even at small scale

geographer – somebody who studies geography or is an expert in geography

geometrical – pertaining to the field of geometry, or something characterized by geometric form or design

globe – Earth; or a map of Earth produced on a sphere

grid system – a *reference system* that uses a mesh of horizontal and vertical lines over the face of a map to pinpoint the position of places. The mesh of lines often helps show distance of locations east and north from a set position. The *zero point* can be any convenient location and is often the bottom-left corner of the map.

hachure – a short line drawn on a map down the slope of hills and mountains to give an impression of *relief*

hard-copy map – a map printed on paper that you can carry around with you

By printing a map of Earth onto a globe, it is possible to avoid the distortions that are found on paper maps.

cartographer – someone who collects information and produces maps from it; the task of making maps is called cartography

contour – an imaginary line connecting places in the landscape that are at equal height above (or below) sea level. The distance of contour lines from each other on a map shows how steeply or gradually land rises. (**see also** Relief)

cosmology – the study of the cosmos (universe) and how it was created

eclipse – the total or partial obscuring of one celestial body by another. In a solar eclipse the moon passes in front of the sun, preventing light from reaching Earth. When

A weather monitoring radar dome at a research station in Antarctica. The southern Polar region is an important location for climate research and atmospheric monitoring because of its lack of environmental pollution.

hemisphere – one-half of the *globe*. It is divided into northern and southern hemispheres by the *equator* and into western and eastern hemispheres by the *Prime Meridian*.

hill shading – the sketching of shadows on the sides of hills and mountains on a map that helps the viewer see the map as three-dimensional

infrared – a part of the spectrum close to red, but detected by the senses as heat, rather than light; infrared radiation is not visible to the eye but can be recorded by some sensors

key – *see* Legend

large-scale map – a map that shows a small area with a lot of detail; like a *bird's-eye view* from a low height above Earth

latitude – a line that joins places of equal angular distance from the center of Earth in a north–south direction. The equator is at 0 degrees latitude, the *poles* at 90 degrees latitude north and south.

layer tinting – showing height of mountains and hills on a map using bands of color to define zones where the land is between two height measurements (between 100 and 250 meters above sea level, for example)

legend – a list of all the *symbols* used on a map with an explanation of their meaning

longitude – a line connecting places of equal angular distance from the center of Earth, measured in degrees east or west of the *Prime Meridian*, or 0 degrees longitude

map projection – a method of presenting the curved surface of Earth on a map on a flat piece of paper or on a computer screen. Different projections use varying kinds of *grid systems* to plot locations.

medieval – the historical period in Europe between 500 and 1500 A.D.

mental map – the picture of a place, its layout, and its linking routes that a person holds in his or her mind

navigation – plotting a route and directing a ship, airplane, or other vehicle from one place to another; we now use the word to apply to journeys on foot as well

oblique view – a view of Earth's surface from above, not looking straight down but at an angle to the surface

observatory – a building in which astronomers work with telescopes and other instruments

papyrus – the ancient Egyptian form of paper made from reeds

parchment – animal skin stretched and cleaned to make it suitable for writing and drawing on

petroglyph – a carving or scratching of shapes and graphical marks on stone; some may represent early maps

philosophy – a set of beliefs about the world; a personal outlook or viewpoint

plague – a deadly disease that spreads quickly among people, especially when they live in overcrowded conditions. Plague is carried by fleas that live on rats.

plotting – making a plan or map of an area; or marking a course—of a ship or an aircraft, say—on a map

polder – a Dutch word referring to a large piece of land, surrounded by protective embankments, reclaimed from the sea by pumping out the water

poles – the points at either end of Earth's axis of rotation where it meets Earth's surface; also called the Geographic North and South Poles

Prime Meridian – the line of *longitude* at 0 degrees; by a historical international agreement it is the meridian line that passes through Greenwich, London, England

Many parts of the Netherlands lie below sea level In order to prevent these areas from flooding, large dikes are built in coastal regions creating large areas of reclaimed land called polders.

Land surveying is vital for the creation of accurate maps. The process is still usually performed by surveyors using instruments such as theodolites.

pyramid – a huge stone tomb of ancient Egypt; a pyramid has a square base and four triangular sides that meet at a point at the top

reclaimed land – land that has been created where a body of water once existed

reference system – a method of recording the position of places on a map so that they all relate logically to one another. Lines of *latitude* and *longitude* make up one common reference system.

relief – the shape of Earth's surface, its hills, mountains, and depressions

sea level – the average level of the sea along the coastline; used as the *zero point* for

measuring land heights, airplane *altitude*, and sea depths

small-scale map – a map that shows a large area with only a little detail; like a *bird's-eye view* from far above Earth

soft-copy map – a map on a computer screen that is not drawn on paper and can be switched off

surveying – the measuring of altitudes, angles, and distances on the land surface in order to obtain accurate positions of features that can be mapped. Surveying the oceans and seas also means measuring distances and angles between visible coastal positions, but the third dimension measured is depth rather than height.

symbol – a diagram, icon, letter, or character used on a map to represent a specific characteristic or feature

terrain – the physical character of an area of land; its *relief*, vegetation, and so on

thematic map – a map that shows one particular aspect of the natural or human environment, such as transportation routes, weather patterns, tourism, population, vegetation, or geology

topographic map – a map that shows natural features such as hills, rivers, and forests, and man-made features such as roads and buildings

vellum – a fine kind of *parchment* made from the skin of very young goats or lambs

zero point – the point that defines the position of all other reference points on a map

zodiac – a division of the night sky; there are 12 such areas covering the whole of the cosmos

zoning – planning what use of land will be made, or allowed, in an area in the future

Further Reading and Web Sites

Aczel, Amir D. *The Riddle of the Compass: The Invention That Changed the World*. New York: Harcourt, 2001.

Arnold, Caroline. *The Geography Book: Activities for Exploring, Mapping, and Enjoying Your World*. New York: Wiley, 2002.

Barber, Peter, and April Carlucci, eds. *The Lie of the Land*. London: British Library Publications, 2001.

Brown, Carron, ed. *The Best-Ever Book of Exploration*. New York: Kingfisher Books, 2002.

Davis, Graham. *Make Your Own Maps*. New York: Sterling, 2008.

Deboo, Ana. *Mapping the Seas and Skies*. Chicago: Heinemann-Raintree, 2007.

Dickinson, Rachel. *Tools of Navigation: A Kid's Guide to the History & Science of Finding Your Way*. White River Junction, VT: Nomad Press, 2005.

Doak, Robin S. *Christopher Columbus: Explorer of the New World*. Minneapolis, MN: Compass Point Books, 2005.

Ehrenberg, Ralph E. *Mapping the World: An Illustrated History of Cartography*. Washington, D.C.: National Geographic, 2005.

Field, Paula, ed. *The Kingfisher Student Atlas of North America*. Boston: Kingfisher, 2005.

Ganeri, Anita, and Andrea Mills. *Atlas of Exploration*. New York: DK Publishing, 2008.

Graham, Alma, ed. *Discovering Maps*. Maplewood, NJ: Hammond World Atlas Corporation, 2004.

Harvey, Miles. *The Island of Lost Maps: A True Story of Cartographic Crime*. New York: Random House, 2000.

Harwood, Jeremy. *To the Ends of the Earth: 100 Maps That Changed the World*. Newton Abbot, United Kingdom: David and Charles, 2006.

Haywood, John. *Atlas of World History*. New York: Barnes and Noble, 1997.

Hazen, Walter A. *Everyday Life: Exploration & Discovery*. Tuscon, AZ: Good Year Books, 2005.

Henzel, Cynthia Kennedy. *Mapping History*. Edina, MN: Abdo Publishing, 2008.

Jacobs, Frank. *Strange Maps: An Atlas of Cartographic Curiosities*. New York: Viking Studio, 2009.

Keay, John. *The Great Arc: The Dramatic Tale of How India Was Mapped and Everest Was Named*. New York: HarperCollins, 2000.

Levy, Janey. *Mapping America's Westward Expansion: Applying Geographic Tools And Interpreting Maps*. New York: Rosen Publishing, 2005.

Levy, Janey. *The Silk Road: Using a Map Scale to Measure Distances*. New York: PowerKids Press, 2005.

McDonnell, Mark D. *Maps on File*. New York: Facts on File, 2007.

McNeese, Tim. *Christopher Columbus and the Discovery of the Americas*. Philadelphia: Chelsea House, 2006.

Mitchell, Robert, and Donald Prickel. *Contemporary's Number Power: Graphs, Tables, Schedules, and Maps*. Lincolnwood, IL: Contemporary Books, 2000.

Oleksy, Walter G. *Mapping the Seas*. New York: Franklin Watts, 2003.

Oleksy, Walter G. *Mapping the Skies*. New York: Franklin Watts, 2003.

Resnick, Abraham. *Maps Tell Stories Too: Geographic Connections to American History*. Bloomington, IN: IUniverse, 2002.

Rirdan, Daniel. *Wide Ranging World Map*. Phoenix, AZ: Exploration, 2002.

Ross, Val. *The Road to There: Mapmakers and Their Stories*. Toronto, Canada: Tundra Books, 2009.

Rumsey, David, and Edith M. Punt. *Cartographica Extraordinaire: The Historical Map Transformed.* Redlands, CA: Esri Press, 2004.

Short, Charles Rennie. *The World through Maps.* Buffalo, NY: Firefly Books, 2003.

Smith, A. G. *Where Am I? The Story of Maps and Navigation.* Toronto, Canada: Fitzhenry and Whiteside, 2001.

Taylor, Barbara. *Looking at Maps.* North Mankato, MN: Franklin Watts, 2007.

Taylor, Barbara. *Maps and Mapping.* New York: Kingfisher, 2002.

Virga, Vincent. *Cartographia: Mapping Civilizations.* London: Little, Brown and Company, 2007.

Wilkinson, Philip. *The World of Exploration.* New York: Kingfisher, 2006.

Wilson, Patrick. *Navigation and Signalling.* Broomall, PA: Mason Crest Publishers, 2002.

Winchester, Simon. *The Map That Changed the World: William Smith and the Birth of Modern Geology.* New York: HarperCollins, 2001.

Zuravicky, Orli. *Map Math: Learning About Latitude and Longitude Using Coordinate Systems.* New York: PowerKids Press, 2005.

Online Resources

www.davidrumsey.com
The David Rumsey map collection. This online library contains around 20,000 historical and modern maps.

http://dma.jrc.it
The mapping collection of the European Commission Joint Research Center. Includes ineractive maps as well as maps documenting environmental and human disasters around the world.

http://etc.usf.edu/Maps/
The University of South Florida's online mapping library. The collection includes historical and modern maps from around the world.

www.lib.utexas.edu/maps
The University of Texas's online map library. The collection includes old CIA maps, historical maps, and thematic maps from around the world.

www2.lib.virginia.edu/exhibits/lewis_clark
An online exhibition at the University of Virginia with information on historic expeditions, including Lewis and Clark.

http://maps.google.com
Google's online mapping resource, includes conventional maps and satellite images for most of the world, as well as street-level photography of Western urban centers.

http://maps.nationalgeographic.com
National Geographic's online mapping service.

http://memory.loc.gov/ammem/gmdhtml/
Map collections from 1500–1999 at the Library of Congress. The collection includes maps made by early explorers, maps of military campaigns, and thematic maps on a variety of topics.

www.nationalatlas.gov
Online national atlas for the United States. Includes customizable topographic maps on a range of different themes.

http://strangemaps.wordpress.com
A frequently updated collection of unusual maps, from maps of imaginary lands to creative ways of displaying data in map form.

www.unc.edu/awmc/mapsforstudents.html
A large collection of free maps, covering many different subjects and regions, hosted by the University of North Carolina.

www.un.org/Depts/Cartographic/
  english/htmain.htm
United Nations mapping agency website. contains maps of the world from 1945 to the present day, including UN maps of conflict areas and disputed territories.

Index